O, WOMAN...
DAUGHTER OF A KING

O, WOMAN...
DAUGHTER OF A KING

30 DAY WOMEN'S DEVOTIONAL & INTERACTIVE JOURNAL

STEPFANIE ROMERO

ISBN: 9798847733137

To my four beautiful girls, Mercy, Meg, Morgan, and Mari. May you never forget to whom you belong and that you are so loved and worth far more than rubies and gold. To my husband, thank you for encouraging me to chase after the things that light up my soul. To my sweet little bestie, my first grandbaby on the way, I love you so much already.

CONTENTS

INTRODUCTION

Do you feel stuck or like something is missing in your life but aren't sure what that is? Are you bogged down with the trials that life has thrown at you and are trying your best to stay afloat to make it through the day? Do you feel alone in your faith walk and are just going through the motions? I understand completely. I've been there more than once and am well aware that as long as I'm on this earth, I'll be met with life's unexpected. However, I have found that knowing my identity in Christ will not only lead me through still waters when a storm arises, but will also guide me to live the life God specifically designed for me.

These daily testimonies of my faith have pushed me to seek Him in everything, and as I do so, I always find me again. What started as journaling my faith walk for my own personal encouragement and healing, motivated me to start my own blog and share my testimony with other women. When I received emails for prayer and thanking me for a message or testimony I shared, I knew it was another confirmation that I needed to write this devotional, something I've been wanting to do for a long time.

O, Woman…Daughter of a KING was written for every woman from all walks, journey, and season in their life. It's intended to encourage, celebrate, congratulate, motivate, and push you to be all that God called you to be. Most importantly, it reminds you each day who you are in Christ and therefore can do all things through Him who strengthens you.

This thirty-day devotional includes a scripture to meditate on each day along with a testimony of my faith that has gotten me through some of my hardest days. I want to encourage you that God carried me through every one of those storms. If He did it for me, He will do it for you.

As a sister, I want to also hold you accountable for not only dreaming about living a life fulfilled, or getting through the storms life might bring, but doing the work to get there. You will be challenged to apply what you've read using the interactive journal. After all, God's word says faith without works is dead (James 2:14). Through this, my hope is that you will be encouraged to know that you are not alone in your faith walk and will feel like you are part of a sisterhood cheering each other on in our faith journey, and to chase after those things that light up your soul and live a life fulfilled.

DAY ONE
DON'T FORGET TO LIVE!

"The thief does not come except to steal, and to kill, and to destroy. I have come that they may have life, and that they may have it more abundantly"
John 10:10 NKJV

This is something I must keep reminding myself to do. I'm a mother of four young adult women and, let me tell you, as they get older, it really doesn't get any easier. Of course, they grow up and become independent, but they still need me, just in different ways. I had my girls very close in age, so needless to say, I was a busy mom. I love being a mom—don't get me wrong—but as I look back, I lost a lot of years of my life. I was so busy taking care of them and making sure all their needs were being met that I forgot about my own.

I sadly don't remember a single time I stopped to look at my reflection in the mirror and acknowledged there was someone on the other side of that reflection, someone that also mattered. Someone that had dreams and goals. It took years before I even stopped for a moment to take a breath and realize there was a whole world around me and my little bubble.

It was as if the years had gone by in seconds. I never saw them coming. It is vital we grab a hold of this message and put it into action. We get so caught up sometimes with the mundane tasks of our daily routines and trials life throws at us, that we are merely existing from one day to the next. Many of us are just trying to make it to the next hour even.

We are like robots following a particular pattern or way of doing the same thing day after day, week after week. We promise ourselves we're going to go here or there, do this or that, but by the time we get home, we're too exhausted to even think about one more thing to add to our plate, so back to bed we go, only to wake up the next day and do it all over again.

Don't get me wrong, daily routines and order are good and imperative for stability in a home. But sister, that's not what life is all about. The Lord said he came to offer us life, and life more abundantly on earth as it is in heaven. He wants us to LIVE and enjoy the life He's given us here on earth. That doesn't always mean that you have to plan some exotic vacation or do some adventurous activity to feel that you're living life. Living is taking the time to step away from your routine to enjoy your blessings. Living can be as simple as going for a long walk and taking in the beauty of

God's creation, or as extreme as going sky diving. Living is stopping long enough to hear what your children have to say, even if it takes thirty minutes for them to finish their story. Living is sitting long enough to rest and savor that sip of coffee instead of chugging it down, to quickly get to the list of all the things you have yet to do. Living is not taking life so seriously and laughing your way through those days when everything seems to be going wrong. Living is taking the time to go on that vacation you've been dreaming about or start checking off that goal list. O, Woman…Daughter of a KING, keep that routine going. Keep being the super woman that you are. Keep moving those mountains. Keep slaying those dragons. Keep being the queen of your home…just don't forget to LIVE!

What can you do today to start LIVING life?

DAY TWO

TAKE THAT LEAP!

"Fear not, for I am with you; Be not dismayed, for I am your God; I will strengthen you, Yes, I will help you, I will uphold you with my righteous right hand."

Isaiah 41:10 NKJV

Somebody needs to hear this. There's someone out there who the Lord has called to start a ministry, launch a business, reach out to a loved one, apply for a new position, go back to school, buy that new house, or move to a new state, but won't take the leap of faith because they're held down by FEAR. I don't know how many times I've stopped pursuing my goals and dreams because of fear. Even this devotional almost didn't make it out because I was paralyzed by fear. It sat on my desk for almost two years without it being completed because I was afraid it wouldn't get published, or worse, no one would read it.

There was another time I wanted to fulfill my childhood dream and become a teacher, but that meant I had to go back to school and get a degree. I put that dream off for years for the fear of failing or not being present enough for my family. I eventually took the leap and enrolled myself in college. Four years later, I graduated with a teaching degree in elementary bilingual education. I later was nominated Teacher of the Year three times. One of those times, I was Texas Bilingual Teacher of the year. I don't mention this to boast but to encourage you that amazing things that can happen in our lives if we pursue those things we've dreamed of and not let fear get the best of us.

The truth is many of us let go of pursuing our dreams and aspirations because of fear of the unknown. Fear of failure. Fear of stepping out of our comfort zone. Fear of rejection. Fear of being alone. Fear of trusting.

O, Woman…Daughter of a KING, I'm here to remind you, "For God did not give us the spirit of fear, but of power and of love and of a sound mind." If you put your trust in Him and allow Him to be your peace and your strength, He will see you through. He is in control of all things, so you can be rest assured that, no matter what, you will become a better version of you. So sister, go start that ministry, launch that business, apply for that new job, buy that house, get that degree, or move to that new state. You've got the Lord before you, beside you and behind you…so, take that LEAP of faith and jump!

What dreams or goals have you been putting off because of fear? What steps can you take to continue to pursue those dreams and goals and make them a reality as you trust God in the process?

DAY THREE
WHEN LIFE GIVES YOU LEMONS, MAKE TEA!

"Do not remember the former things, nor consider the things of old. Behold, I will do a new thing, now it shall spring forth; Shall you not know it? I will even make a road in the wilderness and rivers in the desert."

Isaiah 43: 18-19 NKJV

There are many of us who are going through a season in our life right now where we are being met with dissatisfaction, disappointments, and uncertainty, and all we see is a bowl of lemons to work with, the same bowl we've seen more than we care to. We feel stuck.

Most would say as the old proverbial phrase goes, "When life gives you lemons, make lemonade." Well, frankly, sometimes that same ol' lemonade gets boring.

What if we don't want lemonade? Why not go for the extraordinary instead of the same ol' ordinary? Something different. Something new!

God tells us that He came so we may have life, and that we may have it more abundantly here on earth as it is in heaven. We don't have to settle. We just have to be willing to step out of the box, take that leap of faith, and trust God with the process. This might force some of us out of our comfort zone and even allow fear to creep in because of the unknown.

If you're anything like me, I do not take to change easily. I can remember a time I was so bogged down with the same old routines and wanted to take up a new hobby, something out of my comfort zone. I decided to join a hiking group. I've always loved the outdoors and being surrounded by nature. I mean, don't get me wrong, I was no park ranger that's for sure.

Going fishing and camping out with the family was about as far as a nature activity that I would get. Never did I imagine myself going on long hikes for miles with people I've never met before. But I loved it! It's now one of my regular hobbies, and I've even taken up kayaking too!

O, Woman…Daughter of a KING, you can do all things through Christ who strengthens you. You just have to be ready and willing to enter into a new way of doing things. If you're tired of making ends meet and settling with the same job and have been dreaming of starting your own business, why don't you? If you're tired of living in the same town you've lived in all your life, are ready to move, and need a change of scenery, why haven't you? If you're single and still meeting the same kind of men with the same failed outcomes, maybe try a different approach? If you are tired of the same old mundane routines, why not create new ones for yourself? In other words, sister, if life keeps giving you lemons, stop making the same ol' lemonade. Go make some tea!

What are some things in your life that you'd like to change? What new things can you do to replace those things that have been stagnant in your life and are no longer positively serving you?

DAY FOUR
SO, WHAT GIVES?

"For I know the thoughts that I think toward you, says the Lord, thoughts of peace and not of evil, to give you a future and a hope."
Jeremiah 29:11 NKJV

When we get READY to embrace all God has for us, we must be WILLING to let GO and set BOUND-ARIES for those obstacles that hold us back. Now, I'm not saying to let go of your husband and children. Come on now. However, even with them, we must set boundaries. We must learn to set boundaries with family, friends, work, or whatever may be causing you to remain stagnant.

With some of those things, you'll have to let go and walk away from them. It might be a job, friends, a relationship or decisions you've made in the past that aren't helping you grow and, instead, are causing you stress.

How do you do this? You learn to say no more often to others and yes to yourself. Is this being selfish? Absolutely not! I used to think that by putting myself last, it was the most sacrificial act that a woman could make...as if that made me a better wife, mother, sister, friend, employee, or woman overall.

Although I might have been shining on the outside, with a big smile on my face, listening to those around me telling me what a great friend I was for always being there for others, and what a great mom I was for always putting my children first, I was slowly dying on the inside. I felt lost and numb. These feelings grew and were harder to contain and started to show outwardly.

The things I was doing for others were either done grudgingly or halfheartedly. The truth is, I couldn't give them the best of me until I gave me the best of me. I started learning to say no more often to requests that made me more stressed, and yes to those things that nurtured my soul and spirit.

I started praying and doing some serious soul searching to find out what it was that brought me joy and ignited a spark within my soul. I started running and soon ran my first 5K. I joined a hiking group and recently took up kayaking. I love it! It's brought back a whole new me that I never knew was there.

I even began to embrace the gifts and talents that God had instilled in me and prayed He would use them for His glory. I always knew deep inside that through my writing, I was to encourage women in their walk with God to get through the trials life sometimes throws at us. I just never pursued it. The problem was that it was buried so deep under a pile of "it can wait," "now's not a good time," "sounds crazy," "you're too old now," "what will others think," "it's never going to happen," "I'm too busy," or "someday, I will." But, it can't wait! Now is the time!

Yes, it might sound crazy, but that's what makes it awesome! Stop worrying about what others might think or if you have the time. You'll always be too busy. You never will, until you start today. I'm sure you've heard it a thousand times that we can't love others if we don't show love to ourselves first.

Many of us have bought into the notion that because we are Christians, we are to put ourselves last. That we don't matter. I don't think the Lord wants us to neglect ourselves while we serve others. After all, who can pour out of an empty cup? The Lord clearly says in Matthew 6:22-23, "The lamp of the body is the eye. If therefore your eye is good, your whole body will be full of light. But if your eye is bad, your whole body will be full of darkness. If therefore the light that is in you is darkness, how great is that darkness!"

In other words, make sure you are healthy mentally, spiritually, physically, and emotionally so your light may be of help to those who need you most. I still don't have this all figured out. I'm learning. I'm growing and steadily reminding myself to set those boundaries and to distinguish what those things are that must go so that I can have a clearer path to pursue those positive things in my life. I'm learning to take time to refuel myself by taking care of my own spiritual, emotional, and physical needs before sharing my energy to anyone else. It's vital.

O, Woman…Daughter of a KING, it's time to start loving yourself and embracing the gifts God has blessed you with. Put those gifts to use! Someone out there is waiting to be blessed by them. That someone is also you.

What gifts or talents has the Lord blessed you with to share with the world? What boundaries do you have to place in your life in order to pursue your gifts and talents?

DAY FIVE
WHAT HAVE YOU DONE FOR YOU LATELY?

"For no one ever hated his own flesh, but nourishes and cherishes it, just as the Lord does the church."
Ephesians 5:29 NKJV

If you grew up in the 80s, you might be familiar with Janet Jackson's song "What Have You Done for Me Lately?" Now, take out the "you" and replace it with an "I." Ladies, I can't stress enough how important and healing it is to take the time to do something for yourself EVERYDAY. It doesn't have to be some grandiose activity. I'm talking about doing at least one thing a day that feeds and nourishes your soul and spirit. I'm not just talking about reading the word and praying. Those things are our lifeline. That's how we grow and thrive in the Lord. We should do those things first. I'm talking about self-love and care.

Every day, I make it a point to stop and ask myself "What can I do for me today?" Even if it's just for 10 minutes and it's the last part of the day, I make it a point to show myself some love. It may be going for a drive with the windows rolled down and singing out loud to my favorite tunes, getting a pedicure, lighting up my favorite candle, going for a run, putting in some time on one of my goals, reading a chapter or two from a book I've been wanting to finish, taking an extra-long shower, or grabbing my favorite latte and sipping it in the car savoring every last drop before I go in the house.

Whatever it is that recharges you and brings you calm, do it. Not only will it bring some sanity to your hectic life, but it will replenish and refresh you to be the best version of yourself, for you and for those around you.

Just like a car eventually will run out of fuel if we don't stop to put gas in it, the same goes for us. We must fill up too! How do we expect to be a servant and a blessing to someone when we are running on fumes? Of course, God is the only one that can fulfill our thirst and bring us peace that surpasses all understanding, but He also reminds us that our body is our temple, and we must nourish and take care of it too. O, Woman… Daughter of a KING, now ask yourself, "What have I done for me lately?"

Write a list of things that bring you joy, give you peace, and light up your soul. Now, take the time to bring one each day into your life!

DAY SIX
PUT YOUR MASK ON FIRST

Most of us are familiar with the airplane rule "Put your mask on first" before you help anyone else. When I first heard this, my motherly instinct kicked in and thought, "What? No. I'd quickly put my child's mask on first to be sure they had enough oxygen and were taken care of before me. My children come first!"

Although this may seem like the "heroic" thing to do, or the "mama martyr" title to live by, it's the most foolish. Boy, did I learn the hard way! For many years, I put myself on the back burner. My whole life was wrapped around fulfilling the needs of my husband, children, family, friends, and career.

Oh, it worked for a while. I was labeled super mom, super wife, super friend, super teacher to super woman! However, as the years went by, it was starting to get harder and harder to keep up that image, because on the inside I felt anything but super.

I felt lost, unhappy and even numb. How could I not grasp this simple concept? It's so obvious. If I'm running out of oxygen, I will eventually start shutting down, and I won't be good to my child nor anyone else, and that's exactly what happened.

Those feelings eventually started showing through. I had very little patience with my kids. I would snap at them when they'd ask me a question. I was short and distant with my husband. I stopped replying to my friends and family and began ignoring their calls. My spiritual life was anything but spiritual. I was running on fumes and going down fast.

How did I get to this place? One word...priorities. My priorities were completely out of line. The Bible says to put God first, spouse, children and everything else after. Although not always easy to follow, we get it. The problem is if you read the order of priorities again, where are you in that order? Hmmm...I don't see "me."

That's exactly what many of us miss. We don't include the "I" in the mix. If we dig deeper and see that by putting God first in everything we do, then we will not only find Him, but will find our identity in Him too. He will show you your God-given purpose to start living the life He created just for you.

Before long, you will start living with a new hope and confidence in Him. You will know your worth and will intentionally start being more kind to yourself. You will set those boundaries and make time for yourself too. This is not a selfish act, but a selfless one. By doing so, we are making sure we are spiritually, emotionally and physically sound so that when we do give of ourselves, we do it authentically and with a willing heart.

This is the confidence God gives us when we yield to Him. This, in turn, will cause us to be more willing, more prepared, and more able to be a blessing to others when we ourselves feel blessed.

Sure, I lose my place more than I like to admit. But this only happens when I lose where God's place is in my life. The good news is, I now recognize the pattern and know what I need to do to get myself back in the order of things. I put God first and seek Him in everything, and alas, I find me again!

O, Woman…Daughter of a KING, it's a blessing to serve others and want to be front and center for all your family's needs, but please put your mask on first!

What are some things you can start doing to ensure you have your mask on first?

DAY SEVEN

WHAT ARE YOU DOING IN THE NATURAL SO THAT GOD CAN MOVE IN THE SUPERNATURAL?

"What does it profit, my brethren, if someone says he has faith but does not have works? Can faith save him?"

James 2:14 NKJV

Ladies...how many of us have a list of hopes, goals and dreams that we have been praying for and have yet to see them come to fruition? Our excuse that we say to ourselves is, "It's all in God's hands," and give all the responsibility to God.

But Ladies, we can't put it all in God's hands without first doing what we can do in the natural. I don't know how many times I prayed for things to happen in my life and all I heard were crickets. It's not until I started making moves, when I started seeing doors open, promotions take place, growth in my business, relationships restored, growth in my finances, improvement in my health, and the list goes on.

If I hadn't driven myself to the college admissions building and applied to start school, I would've never become a teacher, a dream that I'd been wanting to fulfill for years. If I hadn't started writing instead of just dreaming about being a published author, you wouldn't be reading this devotional. In other words, God's not going to do what you can do. If you want to go back to school, God's not going to get online or drive you to the university and enroll for you. If you want to start that online business, he's not going to create your website and start marketing your product for you. If you are trying to lose weight, he's not going to go to the grocery store and buy healthy foods for you to eat and then drive you to the gym every day.

You get the gist? God's not going to do what you can do in the natural. When we start moving and do all that we can to get things going, we allow God to do what only He can do. That's when we say, okay God, I did all I can, now it's in your hands. I'm preaching to myself here.

O, Woman…Daughter of a KING…what are you doing to start seeing things move in your life? Yes, the Lord can do all things, but His word also says faith without works is dead. So, let's get out there and put your faith to work!

What is that one thing you have been trying to accomplish but haven't yet because your excuse is, "I'm putting it in God's hands?" What steps can YOU take to get the process going?

DAY EIGHT

EYES WIDE SHUT

"Nevertheless, when one turns to the Lord, the veil is taken away."

2 Corinthians 3:16 NKJV

I don't know how many times the Lord has tried to show me over and over through lessons, trials, and even signs on which road to take when I was stumped about certain decisions in my life. I kept asking friends, read books and articles, and even prayed about it, and still was confused about what to do. But…if I were to be honest with myself, the truth is I knew exactly what I needed to do.

I didn't need a self-help book, nor a friend to advise me, nor did I have to keep praying for an answer. Not that these things aren't helpful. Don't get me wrong. They're important. There's nothing better than being able to call a friend to pray with you and help steer you in the right direction.

Prayer also is a must when making decisions in your life. We always want to be sure God is in the center of everything, and those self-help books, let me tell you, have gotten me through some dark times.

I'm talking about trying to decide on something you already know the answer to. You know the truth. You know the word and you still question. I can't tell you how many times I've struggled in deciding which route I should take when I already knew the answer. There were signs every-where, from a friend sharing a word, the pastor's sermon, a tug from the Holy Spirit to the Word of God, but I chose to continue to walk blindly.

The truth is, I didn't like the answer I was getting and wasn't ready to receive it. I knew I needed to trust God and take His word as it's written and not try to alter it for my own justifications. I knew what the Holy Spirit was calling me to do, but I walked around as if my eyes were wide shut, ignoring the obvious.

Sister, there will be times when we know which route to take that we aren't ready to. That route will hurt, might break you for a little while, cause you to lose friends, or even pull you from your comfort zone. But if you know in your spirit that's what needs to be done, then sister, that's what needs to be done.

O, Woman… Daughter of a KING, I think you know exactly what I'm talking about, so open those beautiful eyes WIDE and shut the enemy from your life.

What are some things in your life that you have been blindly ignoring, knowing good and well that it has no place in your life? How can you change that today?

DAY NINE

CUT THE ROOT

"A good tree cannot bear bad fruit, nor can a bad tree bear good fruit."

Matthew 7:18 NKJV

Throughout the Bible, it mentions the importance of being "rooted" on good ground in order to produce good fruit. If anyone is familiar with planting, you understand that for a tree to produce healthy fruits, its roots must be solid and have a strong trunk, otherwise the roots will deteriorate and so will the rest of the tree.

For a believer, what does that mean or look like? Many of us are walking around sporting the Christian label outwardly, but inwardly we are far from it. How do we know? Well, the "fruits" that we produce in our spiritual walk will tell the tale. I'm not saying you'll be perfect, for the word says, "No one is good, no not one."

I'm saying, as a believer what are you doing to help your growth in your relationship with Christ? I know for me, spending too much time on social media, focusing too much on what's going on in the world and handling things my way instead of God's way, is always a recipe for disaster. I have the testimonies to prove it.

I don't know how many times the Holy Spirit has tugged at my heart about things that were causing a hindrance on my spiritual walk and therefore causing me not to produce good fruits. Sometimes those bad habits come from roots passed down from generation to generation, creating a generational curse in our own family that we must finally take the initiative to say, "No more!"

So, let's step back in our lives and carefully reflect to identify those things that have been holding us back from our blessings and living the purposeful life God created for us to live. At times, we will find there are "roots" in our lives that must be cut off because they are no good to us. They are not placed on solid ground. There are old habits and people that are still connected in our lives that aren't helping our spiritual growth. Instead, they are causing decay, staleness, and deterioration.

Bad fruit might stem from a toxic relationship, friendship, or a job that has run its course, and even old habits. These things must be identified and cut off. As harsh as that may sound, it's true. In John 15:2, it says, "Every branch in Me that does not bear fruit He takes away; and every branch that bears fruit He prunes, that it may bear more fruit."

We must be willing to cut off those roots or branches that aren't bearing good fruit or providing a stable foundation in our spiritual walk, so we can see God's goodness manifest in our life.

O, Woman…Daughter of a KING, that's great news! There is still so much pruning and edifying the Lord wants to do with you, with me. Imagine what our lives will look like, feel like, sound like if we allow Him to show us all the good, He has for us. But, in order to see what that is, we must cut those roots!

What are some things in your life that might be a hinderance in your spiritual walk and causing you not to bear good fruit?

DAY TEN

THE BATTLE IS THE LORD'S

This is what the Lord says: Do not be afraid. Do not
be discouraged by this mighty army, for the battle is
not yours, but God's.

2nd Chronicles 20:15 NKJV

A few years ago, I went through a battle that almost
threatened my marriage. Although my husband and
I were Christians, we grew so busy with the mundane daily
routines of life that we put our marriage on the back burner.
Sure, we were still going to church, praying, attending
Bible studies, and performing all our "Christian" duties.
However, our hearts were so far from the Lord as were our
priorities, and it gave the enemy a free pass to come and
invade and invade he did.

Because I was out of fellowship with God, I lacked

wisdom and was not prepared to go into battle. The first thing I did was try to strategize and come up with a plan to fight in my own strength, but the more I fought my way, the more I realized I was losing fast.

Sure, I prayed, pleaded, and cried out to God, but all I heard was silence. The thing is, as I pleaded with God for help, in my heart and mind I was still devising my own plan of attack. I was not fully surrendered to God's plan and allowing Him to take charge.

Then one day I fell before the Lord completely battered, bruised, and wounded from the battle scars I had incurred from fighting on my own strength. I was like a wounded soldier that could not go on. Then I heard the Lord say to me, "The battle is not yours, but mine." At that moment, I surrendered my plans and stopped fighting my way and let Him have full control.

Sure, I was still in the battle. I held on to my sword (His word). That was my job. As a soldier, I was to use God's word against the plans of the enemy, but I allowed God to fight His way. It was then I saw victory upon victory. I saw the enemy get destroyed right before my eyes, and I didn't have to lift a finger.

My job was to fight with the word of truth, keep my eyes on Jesus and be a light to the ones I was fighting for. Every morning, I would remind myself that God was in control, and I need not be afraid. I taped 2nd Chronicles on my mirror to remind myself what my job was when I would grow weak and wanted to take charge. The more I read it and put it into action, the stronger I became and the sooner I saw the enemy flee.

O, WOMAN…Daughter of a KING, I know life can

come at us with some serious battles to fight, but remember you serve a God who will fight your battles for you. Know your position, be ready with the sword of truth, and keep your eyes fixed on Him.

What battles having you been holding on to and ready to lay it all down for the Lord to fight? Make a proclamation between you and the Lord that you will no longer hold on to these battles, and today you hand them over to Him.

DAY ELEVEN

"SOMETIMES GOD TAKES US THROUGH TROUBLED WATERS NOT TO DROWN US BUT TO CLEANSE US"

"Create in me a clean heart, O God, and renew a steadfast spirit within me."

Psalm 51:10 NKJV

This is so true! A few years ago, I went through extremely troubled waters. My family, my marriage, my health, my finances, and my faith were all tested. I felt like I was in a raging sea with waves crashing over me. I literally felt like I was drowning and every time I came up for a breath, the waves would come crashing down threatening to take me back under.

I came to the point of exhaustion. The more I fought the waves and strategized a plan to stay afloat, the weaker I grew until I could no longer go on...so, I surrendered. Not to the enemy. Not to the storm, but to the Lord!

O, Woman…Daughter of a KING, don't you see…sometimes God allows us to go through troubled waters until the point of exhaustion, until we have nothing left in us but our open hearts before Him. This is exactly where He wants us to be, fully surrendered!

This is the place where we confess all our fears, anxieties, sins, worries, confusion, sadness, and uncertainties and lay it all at His feet, acknowledging that we can no longer do it on our own. We need Him. It is then that the Lord can begin His work in us.

I remember as I fell before the Lord without an ounce of fight left in me, I heard Him speak to my spirit and say, "Ahh… finally daughter, there you are. Now, let me..." At that moment, I felt the weight lift off my shoulders. My troubled waters turned into a calm sea. Sure, on the outside the waves were still crashing and the storm was still raging, but all I could feel was His peace. Before long, I found myself floating with each wave. Not drowning, not fighting back, just riding them through until I found myself on shore again, on solid ground.

Write down a time or two you found yourself in troubled waters. What did you learn from your experience? How did you grow spiritually?

DAY TWELVE
PEACE IN THE MIDST OF THE STORM

"Create in me a clean heart, O God, and renew a steadfast spirit within me."
Psalm 51:10 NKJV

Facing trials in life and trying to maintain some type of calm and normalcy in the midst of it all, can seem almost impossible. When one of my daughters was diagnosed with Thyroid Cancer, I was broken and couldn't function at times. I was terrified of the unknown or worse, losing her to cancer.

I felt like I was drowning, having to gasp for air just to keep going. During these times, all we crave and hope for is for the storm to stop and finally have some calm. However, that's not always the case. At times, we pray and pray for better days, but it seems like the trials keep coming, harder and harder.

Our flesh wants to give up, blame God, hide out, run away, or run to something that might give us a temporary peace, but eventually will only bring about a more crashing and disastrous effect in our lives.

So, what do we do? We take a deep breath, exhale slowly and remind ourselves from who and where our ultimate peace comes from. The Lord is the only one that can give us peace that surpasses all understanding. In other words, even though the storm rages around us, the waters are rising, and the waves are crashing before us, we can still have peace in the midst of it all knowing that the calmer and protector of the storm is in control.

We all are familiar with the Bible story about Peter on the boat. When the storms came crashing, tossing the boat to and fro, Peter was petrified. But God spoke to the winds and calmed the sea! After that, peace...O, Woman... Daughter of a KING, He is God over the storms! You will make it through. Grab a hold of Him, and He will be your still waters. So, let the rain fall!

Search for scriptures on the peace of God. Write them down and refer to them when you feel yourself drowning in the storm. God's word will lift you up!

DAY THIRTEEN
BUT GOD...

"I went down to the moorings of the mountains; The earth with its bars closed behind me forever; Yet You have brought up my life from the pit, O LORD, my God."

Jonah 2:6 NKJV

The Lord has shown me time and again just who He is through some of the toughest trials of my life. I can remember a time when clearly my family was under attack. One of my daughters was in a severe car accident, and shortly after that my other daughter was diagnosed with Thyroid cancer. While they both were in the hospital fighting for their lives, our other daughter was hit by a car, one of our properties was burnt down by arson, and our other daughter decided that maybe college was too much for her and was struggling mentally to keep up, so she took a semester off which would delay her graduation date.

Everywhere I turned, all I saw and experienced were roadblocks, disappointments, hurt, pain, fear, bad reports, and the list goes on. Just when I thought things couldn't get any worse and that I might not make it through another day, I held on to my faith by a thread of hope finding it harder to hold on…but God! But God showed up! But God rescued me! But God reminded me just who He is! But God carried me through! God is the same today, yesterday and forevermore!

My daughter survived the car accident when she was given just 24 hours to live. My other daughter who was diagnosed with cancer is stable and living her best life. Our property that was burnt down was rebuilt back up practically for free, and we sold it for three times the amount we purchased it. The daughter that was hit by a car walked away with barely a scratch or two. Finally, the one who decided college was too much for her, went back the following semester and is now a college graduate.

O, Woman… Daughter of a KING, if you are going through something that is causing you to feel hopeless, fearful, and uncertain about your situation and you are barely hanging on by a thread of hope, do not let go of that hope! Know that the Lord is at work even if you cannot see any light ahead.

It's there, sister! Your "but God" is coming! Remember, this is not the end of your story. This is part of your testimony. It is the part of your life that you can turn back to as a reminder of who God is and what only He can do! If He, did it for me, He will do it for you!

Draw a line down the middle of this page. On the left side write down a list of hard times you've been through, but God brought you through. On the other side write "But God!" all the way down. Let this page serve as a reminder. If He did it once, He will do it again. The Lord is the same yesterday, today and forevermore! Keep adding as you go.

DAY FOURTEEN
SILENCE IS LOUD

"A time to tear, and a time to sew; a time to keep silence, and a time to speak; a time to love, and a time to hate; a time of war, and a time of peace."

Ecclesiastes 3:7-8 NKJV

Many of us might be familiar with the phrase or quote, "Silence speaks louder than words," or "No response is sometimes better than one." Let me tell you, this is hard for me to grasp. I'm a very outspoken person, especially when it's something I advocate strongly for, but God has reminded me many times that although it's okay to say what needs to be said, I need to learn that being silent sometimes makes more of an impact.

Sister, the Lord does the same with us. We could be going through one of the toughest storms of our lives. We are praying, reading the word, attending Bible studies, in fellowship with other believers, going to church, hoping to hear a word from the Lord, but all we get is silence. We wonder, has God left me? Am I not praying enough? What am I doing wrong? Why doesn't He hear me? Doesn't He see that I'm hurting?

O, Woman…Daughter of a KING, those silent moments are when God is speaking to us the most. In those silent moments, He is working on our behalf. He is waiting for us to listen to what The Holy Spirit is trying to say. We can get so occupied sometimes in trying to plead our cause to the Lord that we miss the message. I can't tell you how many times this has happened to me. I've even gotten to the point that I would pray some hard, loud, and long prayers only to get up from my knees feeling empty and worse than before I prayed.

It was not until I learned that there is a time for everything. There is a time to pray and a time to just be silent before the presence of the Lord. In doing so, it gives us the opportunity to hear what the Holy Spirit is trying to tell us loud and clear…through silence. So, sister…shhhh.

What is the Holy Spirit saying to you today?

DAY FIFTEEN

WAIT ON GOD...YOU'LL ONLY MESS IT UP!

"But those who wait on the LORD Shall renew their
strength; They shall mount up with wings like eagles,
they shall run and not be weary, They shall walk and
not faint."

Isaiah 40:31 NKJV

I don't know how many times I must remind myself to
stop making decisions based on my emotions or impatience. I am getting better at it. I'm learning and growing.
How? I take a quick trip down memory lane back to yesteryears for a quick reminder of all the times I decided to do
things my way, on my time, instead of waiting on the Lord.

Oh, boy...let me tell you the consequences were never
pretty! I remember a time my husband and I were having
some marital issues. I saw our marriage and our family

spiraling out of control before my eyes. I went to the Lord filled with anxiety and panic, needing to hear a word from Him on what to do. As I prayed, I clearly heard the Lord tell me…wait.

That's not what I wanted to hear. I pleaded with God. I told Him I had a plan. I knew exactly how to approach the situation. I had it all written out in my head and heart. Then I heard the Lord say, wait. As I stood up from kneeling, I knew in my mind that I needed to wait and trust God, but in my heart, I "felt" due to the circumstances, there wasn't time to lose, so I got up and followed my emotions. I knew I wasn't being obedient to God, but I did it my way anyway. The moment I stepped out of His obedience, I realized I was face to face with the enemy, and I was about to fight a war that belonged to the Lord. But because I didn't wait for Him, I now had to face the consequences of my decision.

His presence and protection no longer covered me. I was on my own, trying to fight a battle that wasn't mine to fight. I was losing fast. It was not until I repented from my disobedience and surrendered my will that I started winning the war.

Sister, if you are at a point in your life or are in a situation where you are trying to decide what to do next, be sure that you consult with the Lord first. If you are already in panic mode or all in your feelings, step away for a bit. Get in the word, in prayer, and ask the Lord for guidance.

Sometimes He'll tell you right away through the Holy Spirit whether to wait or move forward. Sometimes, you might not hear anything from God at all. In that case, just buckle down and keep praying and seeking His will until you do. But whatever you do, don't base your decisions on your emotions instead of God's will or timing. Yes, God's will might not bring instant gratification, and His timing might not seem fast enough. But let me tell you, O, Woman…Daughter of a KING, His will is always perfect, and His timing is always right on time, so wait…

What are some things that you've been waiting to happen in your life? As you wait on the Lord to tell you where to go from here, what can you do to serve and be a blessing to someone as you wait?

DAY SIXTEEN
GET UP!

"To bestow on them a crown of beauty instead of ashes, the oil of joy instead of mourning, and a garment of praise instead of a spirit of despair."
Isaiah 61:3 NKJV

I've gone through many storms in my lifetime, too many to count. However, sometimes they're a great reminder of God's goodness and faithfulness. I give God all the glory for every victory. But sister, I give myself credit too. You see, even though we have faith in the Lord through our storms, and put our trust in Him, we also must do our part.

Our part is to find the strength to keep believing that we will see better days. Our part is to keep seeking Him in all His ways. Our part is to surrender it all to Him. Our part is to keep living when we feel dead. Our part is to search for light when all we see is darkness. Our part is to keep going and find the strength in Him. Our part is to crawl when we cannot stand. Our part is to hold on to the hem of His garment and not let go. Our part is to wait and watch Him move. Our part is to keep running the race knowing that his perfect will await you.

O, Woman...Daughter of a KING, don't give up – or give in. Do your part and Get UP!

What season of your life are you in? Are you happy? Content? Do you feel stuck? Depressed? What are you doing to bring about change spiritually, emotionally and physically?

DAY SEVENTEEN
DIGGING DEEP AND LETTING GO!

"And you are complete in Him, who is the head of all principality and power."
Colossians 2:10 NKJV

How did I get here? One of the hardest things I had to do was admit, acknowledge, and affirm all the things before God that brought me to the place I am today. No matter how bad it hurts or how deep the wounds, we must expose them before the Lord so that all that's left is a white canvas. Even those things that we try so hard to shove deep down from our present and hope they stay there – a place where it's safe and hidden.

It's a place that hides our vulnerability, our weaknesses, our fake smiles, insecurities, anxieties, unforgiveness, and fears. Of course, God already knows all those things. His word says He knows everything about us in Psalms 139.

O, Woman…Daughter of a KING…It's not until we confess those things before Him and strip away all the layers, we've wrapped around ourselves, and are completely transparent before the Lord, that He will then begin to heal our wounds. He'll forgive the sins that have plagued us with shame, and the hurt and unforgiveness we have been holding on to.

Digging so deep within ourselves that we have nothing left but a broken, contrite heart…we will then be ready for all that the Lord has for us so He can remold us to our God-given purpose. Before long, we find ourselves anew, as we let Him remove all those things, we unnecessarily have been holding onto or no longer serve a purpose. New life begins. We start to move and grow as we finally let go.

Have you been holding on to something that has caused you stress, pain, anger, or unforgiveness? Maybe from past hurt from a relationship, childhood trauma, an old habit that has been keeping you from living your best life? Are you ready to let it go? Write it down and leave it at Jesus' feet and start healing, my sister.

DAY EIGHTEEN
WALKING BY FAITH

Now faith is the substance of things hoped for, the evidence of things not seen.

Hebrews 11:1 NKJV

When facing trials in life, we can sometimes lose sight that God walks with us and there is hope on the other side. We become so focused on our problems and situations that any signs of hope seem bleak. So, what do you do? You speak those things as though they were! The Lord tells us that faith is hope unseen.

In other words, even if your situation seems like there's no end, don't accept that. Believe and live your life for those things hoped for. If you get a bad report from the doctor, don't accept that. Start speaking life and healing in your body and live your life as though you were one of the healthiest individuals. If your marriage is falling apart, don't accept that. Start claiming restoration and unity. Keep being the wife that God called you to be. If you've lost your job and can't seem to find another one, don't accept that. Start claiming the job you've always wanted and thank God for opening the right doors.

One of the biggest trials in my life was almost losing one of my daughters to a car accident. I remember the doctors telling us that they'd give her 24 hours. I can't even explain the feeling of hopelessness and darkness that crept up against me. When I saw her for the first time, hooked up to every machine imaginable laying there on the hospital bed almost lifeless, I was so blinded by it all that I couldn't see a way out. I remember crying out to my sister-in-law and pointing out all the machines and how terrified I was for my daughter's life.

Then I heard my sister-in-law say, "I don't see that. I see your daughter alive and well. I see her up and living her life."

I turned and looked at her and thought, she's lost her mind.

But she reminded me of what God's word says, Faith is Hope unseen and that we should speak those things as though they were. At that moment, she and I prayed and started thanking God for healing my daughter. We started speaking life over her and not death. We started speaking all the great things she would accomplish in life and how God would use her for His glory. A few hours later, my daughter did a miraculous turnaround and, praise God, she was healed.

O, Woman…Daughter of a KING, although things may

look like you're walking in a bed of fog and see no clear road up ahead, keep your eyes forward believing and expecting for the light to come shining through.

Write some things down that you have been standing on
your faith to come through. Now, start thanking God for
them.

63

DAY NINETEEN

IS THE WHO YOU ARE TODAY, WHO YOU
WERE CREATED TO BE?

"The LORD will perfect that which concerns me; Your mercy, O Lord, endures forever; Do not forsake the works of Your hands."

Psalm 138:8 NKJV

How many of us are not living the life we were created to live? How many of us go through our entire lives living out someone else's dream or expectation of us? We have forgotten or neglected our own dreams and aspirations because of the fear of not being present enough for our children, husband, job, or whatever the case may be.

We are present for everyone else and are constantly making sure everyone around us is happy, healed, prayed for, or on the road to their God-given purpose or destination, while we're standing on the sidelines watching and cheering on.

When do we step out and jump in the race? Many of us are too busy coming up with excuses that there will always be tomorrow or when the children get older, when my marriage is at a better place, when my finances are more stable…when, when, when.

The truth of the matter is life comes fast as we know it. We soon find ourselves in a place of dissatisfaction, unhappiness, living in regret, and sometimes bitterness. Here's the thing, it's not a "sudden" realization. That's always been there. Many of us wake up sooner than others. The rest of us continue walking around handing out bandages and prize ribbons to those around us while we're oozing with our own wounds and never begin to heal and move forward in our own lives.

O, Woman…Daughter of a KING, NOW is your time to start making those moves and start living the life He created purposely for you. Don't wait another day, make another excuse, or wait for the perfect time. Start living the way God created you to.

Write down your gifts, talents, goals, and aspirations. Now go live a life that matches them.

DAY TWENTY

"IT'S NOT A SPRINT, BUT A MARATHON"

"I have fought the good fight. I have finished my course, I have kept the faith."

2 Timothy 4:7-9 NKJV

Sisters, are you tired yet? I am. But here's the thing, it's okay to be tired. It's okay not to have it all figured out. It's okay that your house isn't spotless every day. As a matter of fact, any day. It's okay if your kids act up in public sometimes or if you dread going to that next Bible study or have to peel yourself out of bed come Sunday mornings.

It's okay if you've rolled your eyes for the thousandth time when you hear your kids yell out, Mom! It's okay if you're annoyed when your husband asks for you to find that one thing that you know is right under his nose. It's okay to be running late. It's okay that Uber Eats is your family's personal chef. It's okay that you just can't keep up with the Jones'. It's okay not to be perfect. It's okay. It's okay. It's okay.

Oh, Woman…Daughter of a KING, this walk of faith isn't meant to be a sprint, but a marathon. Sometimes others might seem like they are way ahead of you in their spiritual walk or overall life, but that's simply not the case. We are all running this race together. Trying to make it home. Some of us might grow weary at times. Others might have to stop for a drink or two to quench their thirst. Some might start the race sprinting and later run out of energy and end up just barely trailing along. Others might be hanging on at the front slow and steady. The point is if we keep going and stop comparing ourselves to each other, we'll soon realize that we are all in this together. Fighting the good fight of faith. Here's the good news. If we hang on and keep going, we all win.

Write some positive things about yourself that you can refer to when you're getting overwhelmed as a reminder to yourself that you're doing great!

DAY TWENTY ONE
WALKING ON WATER

"Did I not say to you that if you would believe you would see the glory of God."
John 11:40 NKJV

I don't how many times the Lord has shown up, shown out, and proven to me that I can walk on water if I just believe. Now, I may not have walked on water like Peter did, but I certainly have experienced so much of God's goodness and faithfulness that I felt like I was walking on water.

I have gone through some trials in my life that I knew only God himself was able to pull me out of. I also have found myself in situations where I've felt insecure in my abilities to do things. One of my dreams was to go back to school and finish my education. I married young and became a mother at eighteen. While everyone else was preparing for college and packing up to start their next education chapter, I was busy preparing for a baby's arrival and trying to educate myself in being a mother.

Fast forward to four children later and, after all my children were enrolled in school, I found myself thinking about that dream again. I wanted to go to college and become a teacher. I sat on that dream for a year more even after my children were all in school.

I routinely talked myself out of it. "I was too old." "I wasn't smart enough." "It's too late." Until one day, I prayed, and God reminded me that I could do all things through Him and that I would get there. I just had to put the work in and believe that I was who He said I was. I could do what He said I could do, and before long, I found myself feeling like I could do anything.

Four years later, I graduated university with honors with a bachelor's degree in Bilingual Education. From that dream, I later was nominated for the Texas Bilingual Teacher of the Year. I was thrown a lavish party at a huge conference center surrounded by my family, colleagues, and wonderful teachers around the state of Texas.

When I arrived, I was greeted by everyone as if I was this famous person. I was even approached by first-year teachers, who I'm sure didn't know any better, asking for my autograph. If they only knew where I came from and how far I've come, they wouldn't believe that someone like me would get this far.

But when the Lord is guiding you and you're living the

life from the plans made purposely for you, you feel like you can do anything. It's like you're walking on water.

O, Woman…Daughter of a KING, you too can be a Peter. Don't be afraid to step out of the boat. Keep your eyes fixed on Jesus and His promises and just believe.

Write down a time that you've felt like you were walking on water after seeing the glory of God move in your life.

DAY TWENTY TWO
IN THE PRESENCE OF MY ENEMIES

"You prepare a table before me in the presence of my enemies; You anoint my head with oil; My cup runs over."

Psalm 23:5 NKJV

I've watched people come in and out of my life who have hurt me. I've witnessed people hurt my loved ones and watch them "get away" with it. I've never understood why people who intentionally bring harm and hurt to others can easily go on with their lives and be able to sleep at night without any remorse.

My flesh wants to lash out and get revenge, but the Lord has constantly reminded me that He has my back and that the revenge is His, not mine. He is always right. Watching God fight my battles for me has allowed me to live in peace, knowing that regardless of who or what's been done against me, the Lord can do far more.

I realized that if I put my trust in Him, no matter the situation or tribulation that I face, the Lord always lifts me up. Lift me up, He has! When I let God fight my battles for me, I find myself feasting before the Lord, basking in His glory as my enemies look on. I find myself victorious at the end of the battle, having never needed to lift a finger.

The word of God says to pray for our enemies. It also says that our enemies are His enemies, and the revenge is the Lord's. Is there someone who has wronged you or your family, and you have been wanting to seek revenge or battling unforgiveness in your heart towards this person?

O, Woman...Daughter of a King, don't let them steal another second of your peace. I promise you, His way is the perfect way. Keep seeking God and let Him fight your battles for you. Before long, like King David, you'll find yourself amidst the glory of God in the presence of your enemies. Here's the kicker. You win.

If you have been battling with unforgiveness or wanting to seek revenge, lay it all out at Jesus' feet and leave it sister. Write it down, date it, and let it go!

DAY TWENTY THREE
WHERE DO YOU GO FROM HERE?

"But seek first the kingdom of God and his righteousness, and all these things will be added to you."
Mathew 6:33 NKJV

Where do you go from here? On your knees…asking God to guide you on the road to discovering who you are in Him. Not who you pretend to be, nor who your parents, husband, children, friends, and family expect you to be, but who you are in Him.

Do you leave that all in His hands and hope one day he'll reveal it to you? No, of course not! God expects you to do those things you can in the natural. You pray and then soul search! Be honest with yourself. Ask yourself what it is you love to do that gets your adrenaline going, ignites a high within your soul that just thinking about it, or being surrounded by it, is like giving your thirsty, parched soul a refreshing, quenchable drink. It brings you such peace and you feel a sense of belonging.

Writing, teaching, and praying for others does that for me. It's as if my lungs give a great exhale, a sigh of relief and freedom. It brings me such peace and joy! Before I wrote this devotional, I started journaling. The journaling was mainly for my own personal healing. Those journals later transpired into a blog. When I started receiving prayer requests and feedback from women all around the world thanking me for sharing my experiences in life and how much it lifted them up, it was so encouraging to me. I felt such a great fulfillment sharing my walk of faith with others. I knew this was to be part of my journey too. It was a gift the Lord blessed me with.

So sister, make it a point in your life to seek what your gift is and use it. Take the time to fill your environment that brings healing to your spirit and surround yourself with people that will cause your soul to say, thank you.

Don't let others' opinions about you or negative talk keep you from your God-given destiny. O, Woman... Daughter of a KING, even if it's an inconvenience for others, do it anyway. Even if others mock you and roll their eyes, do it anyway. Even if it seems unattainable, do it anyway! If God is before you, who can be against you?

We all have one life and were given a gift to bring purpose and meaning into our lives to bring glory to God. Many of us have been carrying around gifts that don't even belong to us or were given to us by someone because they thought that gift was what "suits us" best. Then we wonder why we are so unfulfilled.

The thing is, if we are using the gift God blessed us with and doing everything, we can in the natural to get up and spring it into action, then will you see God do the supernatural. You will feel His peace, watch Him open doors that no man can shut, and see His great purpose for your life. So go seek His guidance and start walking the road that was paved especially for you!

What are your gifts? What brings you joy? How can you use them for the glory of the Lord?

DAY TWENTY FOUR
LAUGH YOUR WAY IN THE HALLWAY

"A merry heart does good, like medicine, but a broken spirit dries the bones."

Proverbs 17:22 NKJV

For many years, when faced with trials, setbacks, or challenges that just didn't go my way, I'd tense up, stress out, and walk around with my shoulders slumped over with an attitude of defeat. Even after the trial passed, I still walked around holding up a wall of uneasiness and anxiety waiting for the next trial to creep in.

I was ready. I had my stern, serious face, fear on deck, anxiety fully loaded with my fight or flight in full gear. But living my life like this was toxic to my soul and my body. Not only was I always stressed out, but I wasn't LIVING my life for fear that something bad was going to happen, so I couldn't relax. I had to stay on guard, so I thought.

What I was really doing was manifesting those things in my life and allowing the enemy to rob me of LIVING life and not just merely existing. I now live my life a day at a time. I try my best to live in the present and not allow the enemy to remind me of the things of old, nor the things that might come.

The word clearly says not to worry about tomorrow for tomorrow has worries of its own (Mathew 6:34). I LIVE for today! O, Women…Daughter of a KING, you might be facing trial after trial and feel like there's no end in sight, but let me tell you, no matter what that trial is, put your trust in Him knowing that God's in control, and that's all you need to know. So, remove that stern look, throw away those fears, and laugh your way in the hallway as you wait for God's next move!

Write two scriptures down that will remind you not to be anxious for anything, but in everything trust God through it all. Refer to these scriptures when your smile starts to fade.

DAY TWENTY FIVE
GIRLFRIENDS

"As iron sharpens iron, so a man sharpens the countenance of his friend."
Proverbs 27:17 NKJV

I've been blessed throughout my life with many friends. The older I get, I realize, it's not the number of friends that makes one blessed, but the type of friends you have that makes all the difference.

I remember a time I was going through a rough time in my life. I had just graduated university and was pretty much broke. My husband and I had recently started our business and were in the early stages of entrepreneurship. If you own your own business, you know what that means... steak or potatoes. We were in a season of potatoes. Let me tell you, it was more than one season. I was also dealing with high anxiety and was diagnosed with hyperthyroid condition.

All the "friends" I thought I had were nowhere in sight. This was a season of hardship. I needed them more than ever. I spent years praying for them, being their cheerleader, and now that I needed their support, I couldn't call on them.

Only a handful were there to walk this journey in my life with me. I am forever grateful for these friends. I learned that a true friend would speak truth to you even if it hurts. A true friend will lift you up, encourage and edify you in your walk with Christ and in your overall life. A true friend will be there to celebrate your highest moments with you and sit with you at your lowest.

I've had to make the tough decisions to love some friends from afar. Not because I'm better than them – I'm always a job in progress – but because they weren't holding me accountable in my walk with Christ, nor edifying my life in a purposeful way.

O, Woman...Daughter of a KING, here's the thing, life is too short. There's no time for small talk, fake friends, or those who really don't always have your best interest at heart, especially your soul. Be choosy and wise in who you surround yourself with. It's better to have one or two authentic friends that love you, who aren't afraid to speak truth to you, than a crowd full of yes-women. You can't choose your family, but you can certainly choose your friends. Choose wisely.

Write down a list of what kind of friend you think you might be to your girlfriends. Be honest with yourself. Those things that aren't "sharpening" your friend's life, work on that. Be that friend that you'd want in your life that reflects this scripture, then expect the same from them.

DAY TWENTY SIX
BASKING IN THE SON

"His brightness was like the light; He had rays flashing from His hand, and there His power was hidden."

Habakkuk 3:4 NKJV

I love the sun. I love the way it warms my face and gives me a boost of energy! I love sitting on the beach, basking in its presence and seeing its rays in all its glory. I love watching it rise and set, bringing me a sweet peaceful, calm.

Now, magnify this feeling times infinity when you experience the glory of our God! I can't think of any other experience or place that compares to basking in the presence of the SON.

I've been through many dark times in my life where I

could not see an end in sight. I yearned for a ray of light of hope to get me through. I was so dry in my walk with Christ that I thirsted for even a small drop of his presence to quench me.

It was at those moments, desperate and completely broken, when I surrendered my darkness to the creator of the universe and behold, His light came shining through. Let me tell you, His presence filled my thirst, warmed my cold heart, made ways in the highways and byways and was my beacon of hope and light.

Before long, the darkness was no longer darkness but a beaming light guiding me through. His rays became strong over me and calmed me with His everlasting peace. I no longer felt lost nor weak, but completely renewed and refreshed, basking in His presence.

O, Woman…Daughter of a KING, God sees you. He loves you. You're not alone in your darkness. Call on the Son, Jesus, and let Him be your beacon of light to get you through. Your suffering is only for a moment. Hang on tight to your savior and let Him be your rescuer too. So sister, get ready, because your gloomy days will soon pass and before long, you'll be basking in the Son.

Are you walking through darkness and need some light? Write down what it is you're trying to hold onto or go through on your own. Now, make a declaration to the Lord that you need His light to see you through, then allow Him to guide you.

DAY TWENTY SEVEN
WHEN ALL ELSE FAILS, KEEP PRAYING

"My flesh and my heart fail; But God is the strength
of my heart and my portion forever."
Psalm 73:26 NKJV

I can't even count the number of times I've been faced with a bleak situation. I mean everything I tried to help the situation only made it worse. The scariest and most heart-wrenching experience was when one of my daughters was diagnosed with thyroid cancer. Her then-oncologist had suggested radiation to help combat the cancer that had metastasized to the lungs.

After several rounds, the results showed no improvement. She then prescribed her an oral chemo drug to see if it would shrink the tumors. Meanwhile, my daughter was losing weight fast and her breathing was growing worse, requiring her to need more oxygen from a cannula.

I was terrified for her life. I researched every doctor that specialized in this type of cancer. I read every medical journal on rare cancers. I prayed and prayed, but everywhere I turned for answers, I was met with more confusion and uncertainty.

We soon met with her doctor, and she didn't know what else to do. I was devastated. I didn't know where or who else to turn to, but God...so, I kept praying. Although everything else seemed like it was quickly failing in every direction, God didn't. He gave me the strength and wisdom to keep searching until He made a way and a way He did!

It took lots of praying and trusting that He was in control of all things, and I needed not be afraid, but believe that He would make a way. I was given the number to the Thyroid Cancer Association to get information on other possible treatments. I expected to hear a recording or given a website for further information. Instead, I was connected to the President of the Thyroid Cancer Association. She was the person that took the call. She just so happened to be there that day answering the phones. Is that a coincidence? No, that's GOD.

She assured me that there was more help and resources available and not to give up. She connected me with MD Anderson Cancer Center and, fast forward to today, my sweet girl is doing wonderful. She now has doctors that go above and beyond to make sure she gets the best opportunity at life. Giving up is not an option, is their motto. Her original doctor was sentencing her to hospice at eighteen years old! But GOD! Since then, she's graduated university with a degree in psychology, is dating a nice young man, the cancer is stable, and she's living her best life.

O, Woman, Daughter of a KING, when all else fails and you see no end or hope in sight, don't give up! Keep praying and watch GOD move.

What have you been praying for? Now, search some scriptures that reminds you of God's promises and repeat them over your situation. Whatever you do, don't give up. Keep praying that God will make a way.

DAY TWENTY EIGHT
WAR ROOM

"Blessed be the LORD my Rock, who trains my hands for war, and my fingers for battle—My loving kindness and my fortress, my high tower and my deliverer, My shield and the One in whom I take refuge, Who subdues my people under me."

Psalm: 144 NKJV

After watching *War Room*, starring Priscilla Shirer, I have a whole different perspective about prayer. I've been saved for more than 20 years prior to watching this movie. But the way prayer was approached, it was as if she was going to war. It really opened my eyes to a whole new prayer realm.

Little did I know that just a year later, I would be setting up my own War Room to fight the enemy off my family.

Like Priscilla Shirer's character in the movie, the enemy came against me to try to kill, steal, and destroy my marriage, our family, and everything God blessed us with. So, I got on my knees and stood on God's word and His promises and went to war.

O, Woman…Daughter of a KING, if you are in a fight of your life, get on your knees, and open the word of God, and speak God's promises over your life and your situation. Remind the enemy who you are in Christ and that the battle is not yours, but God's. Because of that, you already stand victorious!

God's word says everyday put on your full armor of God (Ephesians 6: 10-20). That means be ready to stand firm with The Belt of Truth, knowing who you are in Christ. Your Breastplate of Righteousness will protect you from the enemy's schemes, The Gospel of Peace standing firm on God's word in the midst of war, The Helmet of Salvation knowing that God is your savior and rescuer, The Sword of the Spirit using God's word against the enemy, and The Shield of Faith believing that the battle is not yours, but God's.

Are you going through a fight of your life or know someone who is? Write the names of those people and situations you're praying about and attach some scriptures to them, put on the full armor of God and go to war!

DAY TWENTY NINE

WE ALL FALL DOWN

"But as for me, my feet had almost stumbled; My
steps had nearly slipped."
Psalm 73:2 NKJV

Throughout my faith walk, I've experienced many spiritual highs where I've felt the strong presence of the Lord in my life. God has used me in many ways through leading Bible study groups, praying for women from my women's blog ministry, to being the "go to" person for prayer. I was head of the puppet ministry at children's church and was a Sunday school teacher...you'd think I have it all together, but I don't.

I've experienced many spiritual lows. I've walked in seasons where I felt like I was in the desert thirsty for God's presence and felt nothing. I've prayed for women when I myself was broken and amid a storm. I don't know how many times I have fallen in my faith walk and felt completely numb to it all.

But God has never left my side and loved me through my mess. Just like His word promises, He will leave the ninety-nine to go find that lost one (Mathew 18: 12-14). Let tell you, He has had to go and find me more than I care to admit.

O, Woman...Daughter of a KING, don't you see? If you are in this season of wander or drought, you're not alone. Don't let the enemy make you feel like you aren't good enough or God doesn't love you when you're struggling in your walk. He loves you just as you are. Don't give in to the enemy's lies. You're never too lost to come back and be rescued by God. Keep going, sister! Keep fighting the good fight even when you don't feel like it.

Before long, you'll be back at that place where you'll feel God's presence again and walking that faith walk with confidence. We all fall, but God is always there with open arms waiting for our return and to lift us up again!

Are you in a season of drought? Are you thirsty for more of God but can't feel His presence? Have you backslid? Whatever it is, sister, that has caused you to fall, lay it down at Jesus' feet and get up and hold onto God and don't let go until you feel Him again.

DAY THIRTY

SOMEWHERE OVER THE RAINBOW

"I set My rainbow in the cloud, and it shall be for the sign of the covenant between Me and the earth."
GEN 9:13 NKJV

Remember God's promise to us in Genesis after the storm and devastation from the flood of judgment in the days of Noah. He promised he'd never flood the earth again. The rainbow was a symbol of that promise.

Even after all that had occurred, God showed mercy and grace. Even after the destruction, pain and suffering from the storm that wiped out the earth, the Lord made it so the sun could shine through once again, and life continued.

I love encountering a rainbow right after a storm. It's a wonderful reminder to me of all the storms I've weathered and how God is so faithful!

O, Woman... Daughter of a KING, no matter what storms you've faced in the past or are amid now, stand on God's promises. His word and promises never change. He is the same yesterday, today and forever more! Don't give up or give in. Remember His promise to renew and restore again. Hang on to that, sister, and go look for your rainbow!

Draw a rainbow of scriptures of God's promises and manifest those in your life!

ABOUT THE AUTHOR

Stepfanie Romero is a wife, mother of four beautiful young adult daughters, and a Mimi to four adorable fur babies. She's from Texas and resides in the DFW area. She's a writer, educator, entrepreneur, runner, nature enthusiast, child and animal advocate. She's a former elementary bilingual teacher and blogger of "O, Woman Who Art Thou...You Are a Daughter of a KING."

Join the discussion on the "O Woman Who Art Thou... YOU are a Daughter of a KING!" Facebook group.